DATE DUE

APR 2 8 2008	
MAY 2 0 2008	
JUL 2 2 2008	
NOV 0 1 2012	
OCT 1 7 2014	

GAYLORD   PRINTED IN U.S.A.

21st Century Skills Library

ROAD TO RECOVERY

Karner Blue Butterfly

Susan H. Gray

Cherry Lake Publishing
Ann Arbor, Michigan

CHERRY
LAKE
Publishing

Published in the United States of America by Cherry Lake Publishing
Ann Arbor, MI
www.cherrylakepublishing.com

Content Adviser: Professor David A. Andow, Department of Entomology, University of
Minnesota, Minneapolis, Minnesota

Photo Credits: Cover and pages 1 and 8, A. Rider/Photo Researchers, Inc.; page 5,
Gregory G. Dimijian, M.D./Photo Researchers, Inc.; pages 7 and 13, A. H. Rider/Photo
Researchers Inc.; page 14, Horst Tappe/Hulton Archive/Getty Images; page 20, Gary
Meszaros/Photo Researchers, Inc.; page 21, Larry West/Photo Researchers, Inc.; page 22,
David Hay Jones/Photo Researchers, Inc.; page 26, © Ken Cole/Animals Animals–Earth
Scenes–All Rights Reserved

Map by XNR Productions Inc.

Library of Congress Cataloging-in-Publication Data
Gray, Susan Heinrichs.
  Karner blue butterfly / by Susan H. Gray.
    p. cm. — (Road to recovery)
  ISBN-13: 978-1-60279-040-7 (hardcover)
  ISBN-10: 1-60279-040-X (hardcover)
  1. Karner blue butterfly. I. Title. II. Series.
  QL561.L8G73 2007
  595.78'9—dc22   2007004436

*Cherry Lake Publishing would like to acknowledge the work of
The Partnership for 21st Century Skills.
Please visit www.21stcenturyskills.org for more information.*

TABLE OF CONTENTS

CHAPTER ONE

INSECT BUDDIES

A tiny green caterpillar walks along the stem of a green leaf.

A tiny green caterpillar chews on a tender leaf. The caterpillar is always

hungry and spends its whole day munching away. Suddenly, an ant

runs out onto the leaf. It goes straight for the caterpillar. The caterpillar stays still. The ant runs over and begins to tap the caterpillar. As it does, fluid begins to seep from the caterpillar's body. The ant stops and takes a sip.

Here ants feed on the sweet liquid from a caterpillar.

Karner blue caterpillars produce another material in addition to the sweet, nutritious liquid. When they sense danger, they create a liquid that makes their ants irritated and nervous. Scientists think that the fidgety ants might scare enemies away.

This relationship between the ants and the Karner blue caterpillars is called mutualism. This means that both animals benefit in some way that helps them survive. Can you think of any other animals that help each other through mutualism?

The liquid is so sweet and nutritious that the ant stays and drinks more. The caterpillar doesn't mind. Then more ants come and drink and stay for days. The caterpillar moves slowly from leaf to leaf, and the ants follow along.

And so it goes. The caterpillar feeds the ants. The ants protect the caterpillar from attack. This relationship benefits both **insects**.

CHAPTER TWO

A Butterfly's Life

Karner blue butterflies are small. This Karner blue is a male.

The Karner blue butterfly is a small insect. It is about the size of a

postage stamp. And that's with its wings spread!

Male and female butterflies look quite different on the top side of their

wings. Males' wings are bright blue on the upper side. Females' wings are

The wings of a female Karner blue butterfly are dark blue with orange spots at the edges.

dark, midnight blue, with orange spots along the back edge. The wings of both males and females are fringed in white. On the undersides, both have spots and look the same.

A Karner blue, like every other butterfly, goes through four stages in life. Those stages are egg, **larva**, **pupa**, and adult.

Each Karner blue starts out as a tiny egg. The egg hatches into a larva, or caterpillar. The larva is small, soft, and green. It also has tiny glands that produce a sweet liquid. The liquid oozes from pores in the larva's body.

The Karner blue belongs to a very large family called the gossamer-winged butterflies. Gossamer is a fine, delicate kind of cloth. The butterflies in this family have delicate wings that seem to shimmer in the light.

All family members are very small and fragile. Their wings are covered with tiny colored or shiny scales. Many of the butterflies are either blue or copper in color. Because they are insects, they have six legs.

Like all other butterflies, gossamers have four stages in life. Can you think of some other animals that go through distinct life stages?

All butterflies lay eggs. This egg layer is a common cabbage butterfly.

A larva, or caterpillar, must become a pupa before it can become an adult butterfly.

Ants often come to drink this tasty liquid. Then they stay, even after the larva goes into the next stage. Larvae with ants around survive better than those without ants. The ants protect the caterpillar.

After it grows to its full size, a larva becomes a pupa. At this stage, it

creates a case around its body. A pupa stays in its case for seven to 11 days.

Then the case splits open and out comes a beautiful blue butterfly.

The butterflies must live where there are plenty of plants to feed on.

One plant is especially important to the Karner blue butterfly. It is the wild

blue **lupine**.

Butterflies come out of the pupal case as adults.
This butterfly is a swallowtail.

The blue lupine is a plant with stalks of blue, purple, pink, or white flowers. It grows in dry, sandy soil. It grows best where there is not too much shade and not too much sun. Lupine is found mainly in the northern and eastern United States. Karner blues live in the north.

Karner blue larvae need to eat wild lupines to survive.

A Karner blue feeds on nectar from a brightly colored flower.

Females always lay their eggs on or near lupine. When the eggs hatch,

the larvae munch on the leaves. It is the only food that the larvae ever eat.

The adult butterflies drink nectar from many different kinds of flowers. But

without blue lupine, they would never make it past the larval stage.

CHAPTER THREE

BUTTERFLIES IN DANGER

At one time, Karner blue butterflies lived in 12 northern states and part

of Canada. In the 1950s, novelist and butterfly expert Vladimir Nabokov

first described and named this beautiful butterfly in Karner, New York. But

Vladimir Nabokov inspects a butterfly chart in 1964. This
Russian-born American wrote novels and studied butterflies!

over time, Karner blues have disappeared from Canada and seven states. They remained only in New York, Indiana, Michigan, Wisconsin, and Minnesota. What happened?

The disappearance of fields with lupine is the problem. Karner blues always lay their eggs on or near blue lupine. The caterpillars eat nothing but lupine. As fields with lupine disappear, so do the butterflies.

Several things are causing the lupines to vanish. For one thing, people are building roads, houses, and businesses in places where lupine once grew. Farmers have turned some of the lupine fields into croplands.

A lack of fires is also affecting the lupine habitat. In nature, fires often start when lightning strikes a dry, grassy area. The fires burn the grass, bushes, and small trees. Such fires are actually good for the land. They wipe out scrubby and dead plants and clear the way for new plants to

Natural and controlled fires benefit wildlife in many ways. This fire is a controlled burn of prairie land.

sprout. Fire also adds nutrients to the soil so grasses and lupines can grow.

The removal of trees also helps maintain an environment where the lupine can grow.

Many people work to prevent such fires and disturbances. They worry about fires getting out of control and grass and lupine being burned or torn up.

Although these people are trying to protect grassy areas, they actually are doing just the opposite. With no fires blazing through or trees being removed, young trees have a chance to grow up. As they get larger, their branches create more and more shade. In time, there is so much shade that lupines cannot get enough sunlight to grow. Without lupines, the Karner blues disappear.

Natural events cause the butterfly numbers to shrink as well. Wasps and spiders sometimes

21st Century Content

The Karner blue butterfly became the official state butterfly of New Hampshire in 1992. How do you think this has helped the effort to save the Karner blues?

Insects such as stinkbugs feed on Karner blue butterflies.

eat the Karner blue caterpillars.
Dragonflies eat the adults. Karner
blues also become the meals of
stinkbugs and ladybugs. Very
dry weather can cause the lupines
to wither, and then there is no
place for Karner blue females to
lay eggs.

Destruction of lupine and
butterfly habitat has gone on for
years, and so has fire control. Over
time, the number of Karner blue butterflies
has dwindled.

Karner blues are a great help to plants. The butterflies actually help plants to make seeds.

Before a plant produces a seed, something else must happen. The plant must be pollinated. Some flowers have organs loaded with a grainy material called pollen. Other flowers have sticky organs. Still others have both kinds of organs. For a plant to make a seed, pollen has to land on the sticky organ. Then the contents of the pollen and the sticky organ come together, grow, and become a seed.

When butterflies visit flowers, their bodies pick up pollen. When they brush against the sticky organs, the pollen stays. Thanks to butterflies, flowers can make seeds. And the seeds grow into new flowers. What do you think would happen to plants now pollinated by Karner blues if these butterflies died out?

There are several kinds of rare butterflies in the United States, including Florida's Miami blue.

In 1992, it looked like the Karner blue butterfly might disappear altogether.

That year, the U.S. government said the butterfly was an **endangered species**.

Then, finally, people decided to do something about it.

CHAPTER FOUR

THE ROAD TO RECOVERY

In 1992, the Karner blue butterfly was endangered. But people could not start to save it right away. Instead, everyone needed to learn as much as possible about the insect. They didn't want to make mistakes that might hurt the butterfly population by accident.

The undersides of the wings of male and female Karner blues are silvery blue.

Government workers and scientists studied the butterflies. They

learned where the Karner blues were few in number. They learned where

the insects were more common. They studied the butterflies' habitats.

Then they laid out plans to save it.

One of the first steps to saving an animal or plant is to find out more about it.
This field worker is doing a survey of the wildlife in a woodland area.

Many different groups have become involved in the rescue plans. In Ontario, the Canadian government is working to restore the butterfly's habitat. Zoo workers are learning how to raise larvae. And university researchers are learning the best places to release the adults.

In New York, the Boy Scouts created a trail on their camp property. The trail has signs telling about the Karner blue. The scouts also came up with a new badge. Boys who work to save the butterfly's habitat can earn the badge.

In Wisconsin, landowners helped out. They worked with the government on saving butterfly

Life & Career Skills

After 1988, Karner blues appeared to have vanished from Ohio. But within a few years, plans were underway to bring them back. People at the Toledo Zoo began learning how to raise larvae. And people at Ohio's Kitty Todd Preserve began restoring the butterfly's habitat. In 1998, zoo workers released their first batch of butterflies into the preserve. This was the first Karner blue population to be successfully reestablished in the United States. It also showed how people working together could achieve great results.

habitat. They even planted lupine on their land for the Karner blue larvae to eat.

Even an airport in New Hampshire has helped in the effort to bring back the Karner blue butterfly. Large, grassy fields with lupine surround the airport. Butterflies that were raised in captivity have been released there.

Efforts to help the Karner blue have included planting fields of lupine flowers.

Some plans have not worked out so well, however. In one case, a group gathered many eggs, hoping to raise the larvae. But none of the eggs hatched. In another case, people learned that controlled fires were not enough to restore the Karner blue's habitat.

Although there have been problems, the situation is improving for Karner blue butterflies. Everyone is still learning new things about the butterfly. They are sharing what they know.

Life & Career Skills

At one time, Karner blues lived in New Hampshire. After they disappeared, people began planning how to bring them back. Today, schoolchildren are taking steps to restore the butterfly population. Every year, students grow blue lupine from seeds. They plant the flowers in places that are perfect for the butterfly. They work with a wildlife expert to choose the best places to plant. In 2004, the expert noticed Karner blue butterfly eggs in a lupine field. They were on the very plants that the children had planted earlier.

CHAPTER FIVE

Karner Blues Today

The Karner blue butterfly is still an endangered species, but its numbers

may be slowly going up. More and more people are helping this colorful

insect survive.

The Karner blue butterfly has not yet fully recovered.

One town holds a Karner Blue Butterfly Festival each year. People go there and learn all about the insect. Karner blues have been on television and in the newspapers, which helps educate the public.

At one time, Karner blue butterflies had disappeared from seven states and Canada. They had also disappeared from many areas in other states.

Things are getting better all the time, however. People have planted thousands of blue lupine plants in some of these areas. And they have released thousands of Karner blues. Scientists are now reporting encouraging news. In some places, they are seeing more larvae, pupae, and adults than ever before.

Life & Career Skills

The Kitty Todd Preserve in Ohio is a special place. Every spring, the preserve holds a Blue Weekend. People visit the preserve to learn more about the Karner blues, the wild blue lupine, blue jays, blueberries, blue racer snakes, and blue spotted salamanders. Visitors of all ages observe for themselves the connections between these species in this unique habitat. After all, learning is a lifelong process.

Experts hope that one day there will be plenty of Karner blue butterflies. Right now, they are aiming to have at least 135,000 butterflies spread over 29 different spots. They think it might take until the year 2023 to reach this goal.

Even when that day comes, the work will not be over. The butterfly will still need protection. People will have to remain watchful and do their best to protect the butterflies' habitat. Scientists must continue studying the butterflies to see that their numbers don't drop. There is plenty of work ahead to make certain the Karner blue butterfly is always a part of North America's insect world.

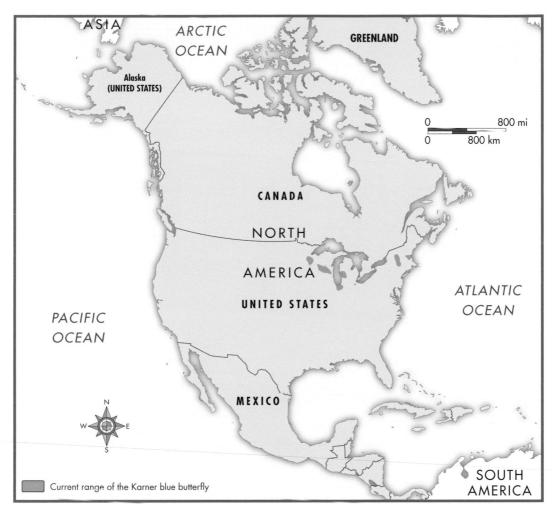

This maps shows where the Karner blue butterfly lives in North America.

Glossary

diurnal (dy-UR-nuhl) active in the daytime

endangered species (en-DAYN-jurd SPEE-sheez) a group of similar animals or plants that are in danger of dying out completely

gossamer (GOSS-uh-mer) a light, delicate kind of cloth

habitat (HAB-ih-tat) the natural home of a plant or animal

insects (IN-sektz) small animals with no backbone, a hard outer covering, three main body parts, and six legs

larva (LAR-vuh) the newly hatched, wormlike form of many insects; also called a caterpillar

lupine (LOO-pin) a plant with stalks of blue, pink, purple, or white flowers

mutualism (MYOO-choo-uhl-iz-em) a relationship in which both sides benefit in some way that helps them survive

pollinated (POLL-ih-nay-ted) brought into contact with pollen

preserve (pree-ZURV) a place set aside for the protection of plants or animals

pupa (PYOO-puh) the stage between larva and adult for some insects

FOR MORE INFORMATION

Books

Boring, Mel. *Caterpillars, Bugs and Butterflies*. Milwaukee:
Gareth Stevens Publishing, 1998.

Latimer, Jonathan, and Karen Stray Nolting. *Young Naturalist
Guide to Butterflies*. Boston: Houghton Mifflin, 2000.

List, Ilka. *Moths and Butterflies of North America*. Danbury, CT: Franklin Watts, 2002.

Opler, Paul A. *Peterson First Guide to Butterflies and
Moths*. Boston: Houghton Mifflin, 1998.

Whalley, Paul. *Butterfly & Moth*. New York: Dorling Kindersley, 2000.

Web Sites

Green Ribbon Initiative—The Karner Blue Is Back!
www.oakopen.org/animals/display.asp?id=218
To read a profile of the Karner blue butterfly and information on its successful recovery

The Nature Conservancy—The Return of the Karner Blue Butterfly
www.nature.org/wherewework/northamerica/states/ohio/science/art20046.html
For information on the conservation efforts of the Karner blue butterfly

INDEX

ABOUT THE AUTHOR

Susan H. Gray has a master's degree in zoology. She has written more than 70 science and reference books for children and especially loves writing about animals. Gray also likes to garden and play the piano. She lives in Cabot, Arkansas, with her husband, Michael, and many pets.